What Can Live in a Forest?

by Sheila Anderson

first step nonfiction

Lerner Publications Company · Minneapolis

A forest is a **habitat**.

It is where plants and animals live.

Forest animals have special **adaptations**.

These help them live in forests.

Birds use hook-shaped **bills**
to open nuts.

Other birds use thin, curved
bills to catch insects.

Ants use strong jaws to cut leaves.

A deer's brown **coat** helps it hide.

Porcupines use claws to climb trees.

They have sharp **quills** to fight off hunters.

Squirrels use long front teeth
to open acorns.

Squirrels use bushy tails. The tails help them land after they leap. 13

These insects look like sticks.
This makes them hard to find.

Bears sleep deeply in the winter when there is less food.

Frogs use sticky tongues to catch insects.

What other adaptations help animals live in the forest?

Bat Adaptations

echoes

Learn More about Adaptations

When flying in the dark, a bat sends out a high-pitched sound. The sound bounces off any trees in the bat's path. The sound makes an echo. The bat will fly around the trees instead of bumping into them.

Fun Facts

 Baby deer have spots on their backs to help them hide among leaves and shadows on the forest floor.

 Hummingbirds use long, thin beaks as straws to drink from forest flowers.

 Monkeys have long arms, legs, and tails that they use to swing from branch to branch.

 Some moths are the same color as tree bark. This helps them hide from forest hunters.

Wolves grow thick winter coats to keep them warm during forest winters.

 Squirrels, mice, and chipmunks use roomy cheek pouches to carry nuts and seeds. They will hide them to eat later.

 Tree frogs have suction cups on their toes to help them grip leaves and tree branches.

 Opossums use long tails and gripping hands to hold onto tree branches.

Glossary

 adaptations – things that help a plant or animal live in a specific habitat

 bills – beaks

 coat – a layer of fur

habitat – a place to live

 quills – long, stiff, pointed rods on porcupines

Index

bill – 6, 7

claw – 10, 14

coat - 9

jaw - 8

quill - 11

tail - 13

teeth - 12

tongue - 16

The images in this book are used with the permission of: © David Combes/Dreamstime.com, pp. 2, 22 (4th from top); © Henrik Alja/Dreamstime.com, p. 3; © Gerry Lemmo, pp. 4, 7, 22 (1st from top); © age fotostock/SuperStock, pp. 5, 10, 14; © Henry Lehn/Visuals Unlimited/ Getty Images, pp. 6, 22 (2nd from top); © Ryszard Laskowski/Dreamstime.com, p. 8; © Rhonda Pierce/Dreamstime.com, pp. 9, 22 (3rd from top); © Alain Turgeon/Dreamstime.com, pp. 11, 22 (5th from top); © Rick Parsons/Dreamstime.com, p. 12; © Cusp/SuperStock, p. 13; © Stouffer Productions/Animals Animals, p. 15; © Mauritius/SuperStock, p. 16; © Vchphoto/Dreamstime. com, p. 17; © Laura Westlund/Independent Picture Service, p. 18.

Cover: © age fotostock/SuperStock

Lerner Publications Company
A division of Lerner Publishing Group, Inc.
241 First Avenue North
Minneapolis, MN 55401 U.S.A.

Website address: www.lernerbooks.com

Library of Congress Cataloging-in-Publication Data

Anderson, Sheila.
    What can live in a forest? / by Sheila Anderson.
        p.   cm. — (First step nonfiction. Animal adaptations)
    Includes index.
    ISBN 978-0-7613-4571-8 (lib. bdg. : alk. paper)
    1. Forest animals—Adaption—Juvenile literature. I. Title.
  QL112.A54 2011
  591.73—dc22   2009025957

Manufactured in the United States of America
1 – DP – 7/15/10